Learning Short-take®

ADULT LEARNING PRINCIPLES 2

Blending interaction with measurement

CATHERINE MATTISKE

TPC - The Performance Company Pty Ltd
PO Box 639
Rozelle NSW 2039
Sydney, Australia

ACN 077 455 273
email: info@tpc.net.au
Website: www.tpc.net.au

© TPC – The Performance Company Pty Limited
Publication date: April 4, 2011

All rights reserved. Apart from any fair dealing for the purposes of study, research or review, as permitted under Australian copyright law, no part of this publication may be reproduced by any means without the written permission of the copyright owner. Every effort has been made to obtain permission relating to information reproduced in this publication.

The information in this publication is based on the current state of commercial and industry practice, applicable legislation, general law and the general circumstances as at the date of publication. No person shall rely on any of the contents of this publication and the publisher and the author expressly exclude all liability for direct and indirect loss suffered by any person resulting in any way from the use of or reliance on this publication or any part of it. Any options and advice are offered solely in pursuance of the author's and the publisher's intention to provide information, and have not been specifically sought.

National Library of Australia
Cataloguing-in-Publication data

Mattiske, Catherine
Adult Learning Principles 2: Blending Interaction with Measurement

ISBN 978-1-921547-02-7

1. Occupational training   2. Learning   I. Title

370.113

Printed in USA

Distributed by TPC - The Performance Company - www.tpc.net.au
For further information contact TPC - The Performance Company, Sydney Australia on +61 9555 1953 or TPC - The Performance Company, California on +1 818-227-5052, or email info@tpc.net.au

HELLO.

Welcome to the Learning Short-take® process!

This Learning Short-take® is a bite sized learning package that aims to improve your skills and provide you with an opportunity for personal and professional development to achieve success in your role.

This Learning Short-take® combines self study with workplace activities in a unique learning system to keep you motivated and energized. So let's get started!

Step 1:
What's inside?

- Learning Short-take® Participant Guide. This section contains all of the learning content and will guide you through the learning process.
- Learning Activities. You will be prompted to complete these as you read through the Participant Guide.
- Learning Journal. This is a summary of your key learnings. Update it when prompted.
- Skill Development Action Plan. Learning is about taking action. This is your action plan where you'll plan how you will implement your learning.

Step 2:
Complete the Learning Short-take®

- Learning Short-takes® are best completed in a quiet environment that is free of distractions.
- Schedule time in your calendar to complete the Learning Short-take® and prioritize this time as an investment in your own professional development.
- Depending on the title, most participants complete the Learning Short-take® from 90 minutes to 2.5 hours.

Step 3:
Meet with your Manager/Coach

- Schedule a 30 minute meeting with your Manager or Coach.
- At this meeting share your completed Activities, Learning Journal and Skill Development Action Plan.
- Most importantly, discuss and agree on how you will implement your learning in your role.

Welcome

Adult Learning Principles 2
Blending Interaction with Measurement

Adult Learning Principles 2 combines self-study with realistic workplace activities to develop skills in learning measurement. Building on Adult Learning Principles 1, this Learning Short-take® examines the importance of Return on Investment (ROI) in training and explores common myths around learning measurement. For trainers, educators, facilitators and managers the library of training activities will allow you to develop new and innovative strategies to assess learning during workshops, training programs and e-Learning sessions.

In the world of training and development, the subject of measuring ROI is discussed frequently. Organizations everywhere are searching for the perfect measurement system to link human resource capability with the business strategy. To achieve this result, it is important to understand how learning can be effectively measured in the classroom. It is during the training itself that we have the first opportunity to observe learning transfer taking place.

Adult Learning Principles 2 provides a library of 18 training activities that can be used to measure learning during training courses. It also includes the **Training Review Analysis** tool, provided as a free download.

Now let's get started!

1	Participant Guide > Start here
2	Learning Journal 65
3	Skill Development Action Plan 71
4	Quick Reference 77
5	Next Step 99

> "You don't understand anything until you learn it more than one way."
>
> Marvin Minsky

"You can teach a student a lesson for a day; but if you can teach him to learn by creating curiosity, he will continue the learning process as long as he lives."

Clay P. Bedford

Section 1

PARTICIPANT GUIDE

Start here

What's in this Participant Guide?

"The most useful piece of learning for the uses of life is to unlearn what is untrue."

Antisthenes

Table of Contents

How to Complete Your Learning Short-take®	5
Activity Checklist	6
Learning Objectives	7
Let's Get Started	8
Part 1 - Understanding ROI	9
The Importance of ROI (Return on Investment) in Training	10
Part 2 - Measurement Myths	17
Common Myths About Measuring Training in the Classroom	18
Part 3 - Kirkpatrick's Model	25
Kirkpatrick's Learning Evaluation Model	26
Part 4 - Measuring through Review	37
The "Review" as a Solid Training Measure	38
Types of Review Activities	43
12 More Review Activities	51
Different Levels of Review	55
Balancing Adult Learning Styles	58
Part 5 - Bringing it Together	61

How to Complete Your Learning Short-take®

1. **Reflect on your skills and abilities** for measuring the effectiveness of learning, and how well you use these skills to achieve success in training.

2. **Complete the Initial Skills Assessment.**

3. Highlight specific skill areas that you believe you could develop more. Add these to the **Learning Journal.** Add to your Learning Journal as you go.

4. When you have completed this Learning Short-take® **meet with your Manager/Coach.** In this meeting, you will jointly establish a personal **Skill Development Action Plan.**

5. **Subject to your coach's final review** and assessment, you will either sign off the module, or undertake further skill development as appropriate.

"You learn something every day if you pay attention."

Ray LeBlond

Activity Checklist

1

"A single conversation with a wise man is better than ten years of study."

Chinese Proverb

During this Learning Short-take® you will be prompted to complete the following activities:

- Activity 1 - Initial Skill Assessment   14
- Activity 2 - Feedback Hit or Myth   22
- Activity 3 - The Learning Evaluation Model   35
- Activity 4 - Case Study   41
- Activity 5 - Training Review Analysis   60
- Activity 6 - Quick Tips   63
- Learning Journal   65
- Skill Development Action Plan   71

Learning Objectives

Once you have completed this Learning Short-take®, you should be able to:

- Explain the importance of ROI (Return on Investment) in training
- Identify common myths about measuring training in the classroom
- Explain Kirkpatrick's Learning Evaluation Model
- Explain the value of Review as a solid training measurement
- Describe the various types of Reviews
- Identify and explain the different levels of Review
- Create a Skill Development Action Plan

"Some people will never learn anything, for this reason, because they understand everything too soon."

Alexander Pope

Let's Get Started

In the world of training and development, the subject of measuring return on investment (ROI) is discussed frequently. It seems that organizations everywhere are searching for the perfect measurement system to link human resource capability with the business strategy.

Senior executives, Organizational Development Consultants, Training Managers and Human Resource Practitioners agree that learning and development activity must have an impact on the bottom line.

To facilitate a positive bottom-line result, it is important to first understand how learning can be effectively measured in the classroom. It is during the training event itself that we have the first opportunity to observe learning transfer taking place. If learning transfer can be managed and measured in the classroom, then there is real opportunity to measure workplace application and contribution to organizational results.

This Learning Short-take® combines self-study with workplace activities to develop skills in learning measurement. Participants will examine the importance of ROI in training and explore common myths around learning measurement. Participants will learn practical tools and develop new and innovative strategies to assess learning in the classroom.

tpc

UNDERSTANDING ROI

Part 1

The Importance of ROI (Return on Investment) in Training

"Organizations expect that learning from a training course will be transferred to the workplace."

Catherine Mattiske

The issue of return on investment (ROI) in training and development has become a critical challenge for learning and development professionals. Organizations pay, either directly or indirectly, for their people to attend training.

In return they expect to see learning goals achieved and a corresponding behavior change in those who attended.

Furthermore, they expect this behavior change to have a positive impact on the performance of the business.

ROI has become a hot topic in the training and development arena for a number of reasons:

1. HRD (Human Resource Development) budgets have continued to grow, and as expenditure grows, so too does accountability. Budget increases draw the attention of internal critics who force the development of ROI evaluation.

2. The trend on total quality management and continuous improvement processes has heightened attention on the issue of measurement. Organizations are now more conscious of measuring processes and outputs that were previously left unchecked. The increased measurement focus has placed pressure on the training and development and HR function to develop measures of its outputs and successes.

3. The rise in restructuring and outsourcing activities has redirected the attention of HR and training specialists to the bottom line. Under scrutiny from the rest of the organization, the training and development function is now focused on actively linking learning programs to business needs and organizational efficiencies.

4. The business management mindset of current training and HR managers leads them to place more emphasis on economic issues within the learning function. Today's training manager is more aware of bottom-line issues in the organization and is more knowledgeable of the operational and financial business parameters.

5. Accountability has been a consistent trend for all functions in the organization. Each support function is attempting to show its worth by trying to measure the value it adds to the organization. Like all functions, learning and development must show its contribution.

Reasons for Measuring Training and Development Activities

1. Organizational Level

There are a number of compelling reasons why organizations should measure the contribution of the learning function, and the progress of the training and development curriculum.

- To make sure that training and development initiatives are taking the organization in the right direction.
- To determine whether the actions being taken or behavior changes resulting from the training align with the business expectations and performance standards.
- To justify the costs of training and development initiatives that were developed to enhance organizational performance.
- To provide base-line measurements that can identify favorable or unfavorable trends with respect to training initiatives and the organization's goals and objectives.

2. Classroom Level

Transfer of learning in the classroom is our first opportunity to observe how well the learning might be applied back in the workplace. If there is no measurement of learning during the program itself, it is impossible to determine how well participants have understood the content, or how confident they are to apply what has been learned on the job.
The program becomes simply a 'training event' with no real alignment to the performance expectations of participants, or the impact on business results.

The ability to measure learning during training is critical to the bigger picture of measuring the impact of corporate training initiatives. Only when the trainer can observe and measure learning transfer in the classroom is there opportunity to provide real and useful data back to the organization. As this Learning Short-take® develops we will continue to explore opportunities for measuring learning in the classroom.

Complete Activity # 1
Initial Skills Assessment

Activity 1: Initial Skills Assessment

Understanding how to measure learning in the classroom is critical to training and organizational success. This assessment covers the key skills for measuring learning in order to improve learning outcomes and workplace application.

Rate yourself on each of the techniques.
7 is competent and confident, little need for improvement
4 is average, needs improvement
1 is uncomfortable, major need for improvement

- Note specific areas of improvement related to each skill that you would like to develop. Be sure to include your *reasons* for your rating in each skill.

When conducting training programs and providing feedback to participants, I…	Rating	Reasoning
am confident that my participants leave the room with the knowledge and capability to implement what has been learnt.	1 2 3 4 5 6 7	
never rely on evaluation forms as a measurement of learning success.	1 2 3 4 5 6 7	
never use tests or exams as a measure of learning.	1 2 3 4 5 6 7	
always incorporate review activities into my training programs.	1 2 3 4 5 6 7	
delete content rather than a review if I am running short of time in a program.	1 2 3 4 5 6 7	
do not design my review activities based purely on fun, but rather a genuine review of content to measure participant understanding.	1 2 3 4 5 6 7	
understand the difference between a training activity and a review activity.	1 2 3 4 5 6 7	
plan the duration of my reviews based on the volume of content being assessed to ensure appropriate use of time.	1 2 3 4 5 6 7	
always debrief a review activity.	1 2 3 4 5 6 7	

Activity 1: Continued

When conducting training programs and providing feedback to participants, I…	Rating	Reasoning
use a variety of review types to cater to the different adult learning styles in the room.	**1** 2 3 4 5 6 7	
use a variety of review levels to engage participants on an individual, team, and whole group level.	**1** 2 3 4 5 6 7	
have a defined learning expectation for every review activity that I run.	**1** 2 3 4 5 6 7	
use reviews to measure learning of both conceptual information and step-by-step process information.	**1** 2 3 4 5 6 7	

Personal development plan ideas:

1

2

Now update your Learning Journal (page 65)

1

"The beautiful thing about learning is nobody can take it away from you."

B. B. King

MEASUREMENT MYTHS

Part 2

Common Myths About Measuring Training in the Classroom

1

There are four common myths surrounding the measurement of learning in the classroom:

Myth 1: Learning Can't be Measured During a Training Course

For a trainer to know that participants are capable of applying new skills and ideas in the workplace, measurement must take place during the course.

Before participants leave the room, the trainer must be confident that they have the knowledge and capability to implement what has been learned. Measuring learning during a program is about creating regular opportunities for participants to test-drive their new skills. Through a combination of semi-guided and unguided activities, the participant is able to fully explore the learning as it relates to their work. Through effective feedback and debrief of activities the trainer can measure participant confidence and competence, and the odds of successful learning transfer to the workplace are greater. Furthermore, post-course evaluation and measurement becomes richer and more valuable.

Myth 2: A Written Test or Exam Measures Learning

In recent years much has been written about how adults learn. At the core of this research is the notion that adults do/do not learn simply because they pass or fail an exam. What the exam really tests is how well an adult remembers and regurgitates facts about a particular subject. Professional trainers know that some adults do well at exams and others do not. Furthermore, the results are not a true indication of how much learning has taken place. Rarely does the exam environment mirror the environment in which the learning will be applied. On the job, participants have several options to finding solutions to a problem – reference material, help desks, training aids, internal and external networks etc. Exams and tests only measure what is remembered on the day, not necessarily what has been learned.

Myth 3: An Evaluation Form is a Measure of Learning

It is the expectation of many organizations that evaluation forms adequately measure trainer competence, the content of the course, and how much learning has taken place. However, depending on the content of the evaluation, the form may not measure these things at all. Evaluation forms generally evaluate the execution of the training course, its administration, and perhaps even the trainer and the content presented, but they do not measure learning. It is well known fact that evaluation forms are often referred to as 'smile sheets'. Participants are generally gracious people who have been taught not to hurt the feelings of others. They know that the trainer will read the evaluation form and they believe that regardless of the trainer's skill and competence, the trainer probably tried their best. If the trainer is internal to the organization then participants are even more likely to provide a positive evaluation as they may know or even work with the trainer now or in the future.

If a participant did not enjoy the program, or did not understand the content, they are also not likely to reveal this on an evaluation form. They will generally leave sections of the form blank if they have nothing positive to say.

Myth 4: There is no time left in the course for review

For any professional trainer, the goal at the end of the program is that participants know 100% or close to it, of all the topics covered. The only way this can be assessed is through ongoing review activities to help the trainer observe participant competence and confidence in the use of new skills. To incorporate an appropriate quantity and quality of review time in any program a choice must be made between the volume of content presented and learning measurement. The bottom line is that you cannot afford not to have review activities. If your purpose is to have skilled participants who are ready to apply their learning on the job, you will create time for reviews. If you run short of time it is better to drop content before dropping a review. It is better for participants to have an opportunity to road test their skills, than to be confused and overwhelmed by a mass of content.

"We learn more by looking for the answer to a question and not finding it than we do from learning the answer itself."

Lloyd Alexander

Complete Activity # 2
Feedback Hit or Myth

Activity 2: Feedback Hit or Myth

1 Are the following statements about feedback true (Hit) or false (Myth)?

	Hit	Myth	If Myth, why?
1. It is not possible to measure learning during a training course.			
2. Before participants leave the room, the trainer must be confident that participants have the skills and knowledge to implement what has been learned.			
3. A written test or exam provides a good indication of learning transfer.			
4. Evaluation forms are an adequate measure of trainer competence, course content, and how much learning has taken place.			
5. For any professional trainer, the goal at the end of the program is that participants know all or most of the topics covered.			
6. If you run short of time, it is better to drop content than drop a review activity.			
7. An exam tests how well participants can remember and regurgitate facts about a particular subject.			

Activity 2: Continued

		Hit	Myth	If Myth, why?
8.	When review activities are used regularly throughout a training program, post-course evaluation and measurement becomes richer and more valuable.			
9.	Evaluation forms are often referred to as 'smile sheets'.			
10.	In any training program it is critical that participants receive all the information they need, even if this means they have to practice new skills at a later date.			
11.	If there is time pressure, it is better to skip a review debrief than to lose a review activity altogether.			
12.	Participants are more likely to give an internal trainer a fabulous review because they know them and may work with them now or in the future.			
13.	Participants will leave sections of an evaluation form blank if they have not understood content, or if they have nothing positive to say.			

Activity # 2 - Check your Answers

Check your work from the previous activity.

Statement	Hit or Myth	If Myth, Why?
It is not possible to measure learning during a training course.	Myth	Measurement must take place during the course. This is achieved through a combination of guided and semi-guided review activities.
Before participants leave the room, the trainer must be confident that participants have the skills and knowledge to implement what has been learned.	Hit	
A written test or exam provides a good indication of learning transfer.	Myth	Adults do not learn simply because they pass or fail an exam.
Evaluation forms are an adequate measure of trainer competence, course content, and how much learning has taken place.	Myth	Evaluation forms do not measure learning They generally evaluate the execution and administration of the course.
For any professional trainer, the goal at the end of the program is that participants know all or most of the topics covered.	Hit	
If you run short of time, it is better to drop content than drop a review activity.	Hit	It is better to review and check understanding than overwhelm participants with content.
An exam tests how well participants can remember and regurgitate facts about a particular subject.	Hit	
When review activities are used regularly throughout a training program, post-course evaluation and measurement becomes richer and more valuable.	Hit	
Evaluation forms are often referred to as 'smile sheets'.	Hit	
In any training program it is critical that participants receive all the information they need, even if this means they have to practice new skills at a later date.	Myth	Skill must be road-tested soon after new information has been presented ie. on the day.
If there is time pressure, it is better to skip a review debrief than to lose a review activity altogether.	Myth	The debrief is critical to the success of the review activity and in ensuring that learning transfer has taken place.
Participants are more likely to give an internal trainer a fabulous review because they know them and may work with them now or in the future.	Hit	
Participants will leave sections of an evaluation form blank if they have not understood content, or if they have nothing positive to say.	Hit	

Now update your Learning Journal (page 65)

KIRKPATRICK'S MODEL

Part 3

Kirkpatrick's Learning Evaluation Model

Donald L Kirkpatrick's theory on evaluation (Evaluating Training Programs. 1959) has arguably become the most widely used and popular model for the evaluation of training and learning. Kirkpatrick's four-level model is now considered an industry standard across the HR and training communities. The four levels of training model was later redefined and updated in Kirkpatrick's 1998 book, called *Evaluating Training Programs: The Four Levels*.

Level	Evaluation Type (what is measured)	Evaluation Description and Characteristics	Examples of Evaluation Tools and Methods	Relevance and Practicability
1	reaction	• reaction evaluation is how the delegates felt about the training or learning experience	• eg., 'happy sheets', feedback forms • also verbal reaction, post-training surveys or questionnaires	• quick and very easy to obtain • not expensive to gather or to analyze
2	learning	• learning evaluation is the measurement of the increase in knowledge – before and after	• typically assessments or tests before and after the training • interview or observation can also be used	• relatively simple to set up; clear-cut for quantifiable skills • less easy for complex learning
3	behavior	• behavior evaluation is the extent of applied learning back on the job – implementation	• observation and interview over time are required to assess change, relevance of change, and sustainability of change	• measurement of behavior change typically requires cooperation and skill of line-managers
4	results	• results evaluation is the effect on the business or environment by the trainee	• measures are already in place via normal management systems and reporting – the challenge is to relate these to the trainee	• individually not difficult; unlike whole organization • process must attributing clear accountabilities

Level 1: Reactions and Planned Action

Question: How did participants respond to the training?

Reaction measures, also known as evaluation forms or "smile sheets" are the most commonly used type of evaluation. Reaction measures assess how participants responded to the training class, event, or materials.

Warr and Bruce (1995) describe three kinds of reactions that are measured:

- Enjoyment of training *(emotional reaction)* - "I found this training program to be enjoyable."
- Usefulness of training *(perceived value)* - "What level of value does the training content have for your job?"
- Difficulty of training - "I found the issues taught in training difficult to understand."

This information is usually collected immediately after the training is completed. Reaction measures are usually fairly brief, but can go into great depth about any of the issues described above.

"I am always ready to learn although I do not always like being taught."

Winston Churchill

Level 2: Learning

1

Question: To what extent did participants experience changes in attitudes, skills, or motivations as a result of the training?

Learning can be defined and assessed in many ways. For example, we could measure participants' ability to answer questions about the training content, or their ability to demonstrate newly acquired skills. Kurt Kraiger and his colleagues (1993) identified three types of learning that might result from training:

- **Cognitive Outcomes** – Usually assessed by multiple choice questions, open-ended responses, listing of facts, or similar methods. Knowledge checks such as these are very similar to tests used in schools to assign grades. Measures of cognitive outcomes can be assessed immediately after training or later to assess knowledge retention over time.

- **Skill-Based Outcomes** – These outcomes are typically measured by requiring that participants demonstrate their new skills in the training environment. Skill-based outcomes are not the same as behavior-change outcomes (Level 3) that occur in the work environment. Learning outcomes that focus on skills only measure participants' ability to demonstrate the skills.

- **Attitudinal Outcomes** – These measures focus on how participants feel or think about the training content. They have implications for participants' motivation to use the training, their confidence for using the skills, and their ability to reach goals.

To determine whether learning has occurred, we could compare pre-/post-performance to learning measures. Having a control group also helps us draw conclusions by allowing us to compare the performance of trained and untrained individuals.

Level 3: Behavior

Question: Can behavior change be observed on the job as a result of training (i.e., learning transfer)?

Level 3 is all about how participants use their skills or apply their new knowledge in the workplace. In most cases, training success is defined in terms of behavior change. However, Level 3 focuses on what happens to training participants after they leave the training environment. At this point, we are focusing on training effectiveness and not training evaluation. Measures used at Levels 1 and 2 are associated only with the influence of the training. If results are positive or negative, we can usually point to the training as the primary cause. Levels 3, 4, and 5 include the influences of many factors besides the content of the training or its delivery. Measuring behavior change usually requires some type of pre-/post-training assessment. Often, this type of assessment comes in the form of a multi rater (i.e., 360 degree) assessment. Performance management systems have also been used to track changes in performance before and after training.

However, this approach requires a carefully structured performance management system that keeps accurate records of participants' accomplishments. There are other methods of measuring behavior change, but they are often not practical. For example, observing training participants on the job and monitoring their performance with checklists. Or tracking the number of errors they make when using skills taught in training. Multi rater assessments can be easily administered, and provide a quick read on skill application. Ideally, a control group should be used to add validity to the findings.

Level 4: Results

Question: How have organizational outcomes changed as a result of the training program?

By far, Level 4 is the most difficult training outcome to measure. "Results" can include almost any criteria by which organizational success is defined. These measurements are linked to the organization's business case, critical success factors, or strategic objectives.

Examples of results might include:

- Productivity
- Customer satisfaction
- Efficiency
- Morale
- Profitability

"I have never in my life learned anything from any man who agreed with me."

Dudley Field Malone

These outcomes are usually tracked over time (e.g., month to month) or measured before and after the training. Changes in results might appear in the form of significant deviations in long-term trends or sudden jumps in monthly measures. Unfortunately, it is not always clear how long it will take for a training intervention to have an impact on organizational results. Changes could occur immediately or appear years later. As in any study, measuring parallel results from a control group adds validity to the conclusions.

Even though business results are the most removed from training, they often receive the most attention. Sometimes so many factors interfere with the influence of training that it might appear that training has no real effect on the bottom line.

Numerous researchers have made the point that it is not appropriate to evaluate training at Level 4. The uncontrolled, non-laboratory setting of organizations makes it almost impossible to isolate the impact of any one program.

In Level 4, we assume that if organizations train and develop people, they should realize positive bottom-line outcomes. Measuring the effectiveness of training and development curriculums at this level can be an expensive, time-consuming drain of resources. Before undertaking this level of measurement, an organization must carefully consider whether it is cost effective and warranted.

"Beware of the man who works hard to learn something, learns it, and finds himself no wiser than before."

Kurt Vonnegut, Jr.

Level 5: Return on Investment (ROI) - Jack Phillips

Question: Did the benefits of training outweigh the costs?

By focusing on a calculated percentage return, Level 5 is distinct from the more generic Level 4. Level 5 is an "add-on" from Jack Phillips.

It measures the cost of the training intervention versus the return on investment. Usually, gains observed from the training intervention (such as changes in results or behavior change) are converted into monetary values. These returns are then compared to the per-person cost of the training. Many factors are used to calculate ROI, and entire books have been written to explain the process (also known as utility analysis). For example, ROI must account for the fact that money spent on training could have been invested in other company ventures.

Therefore, training must not only return its costs, it must exceed the potential value of alternative investments. Although most OD managers or training and development managers would love to calculate these measures, they are difficult to obtain and explain. Attempting to show cause-and-effect relationships between training and ROI takes expertise and patience. In the end, the benefit of calculating and presenting a complex estimation of value must outweigh the costs of preparing such information.

Measurement Criteria

Here are some criteria to consider when identifying the measures of effectiveness for training and development curriculums:

- Measurement systems must be easy to understand by everyone involved.

- Decide what you are going to do with the data you gather. Are you going to distribute it? Is it going to be part of a presentation?

- Manage your internal customers' expectations. Make sure they are comfortable with the type of data you are collecting and will have confidence in the results.

- Before deciding on which measurements to use, identify the business needs. What is the root problem that is driving the training?

- Identify the objectives of the training curriculum for the short-term and the long term. Where should you see immediate versus long-term effects?

- Candidly discuss any barriers, drivers, or constraints to implementing the training and development curriculum (i.e., resources, level of investment, other concurrent initiatives, etc.).

- Define the audience levels of employees who will benefit from the training (number of employees, location, shift, etc.). How will the training affect these breakouts?

- Link the business strategy and cultural strategy to the training and development curriculum. How does the training support the strategy?

- Allow the measurement systems to be influenced by those making the decisions. If you don't involve your primary customers in the design of the measurements, they will be less likely to accept the results.

- Decide whether your measures will be "one shot" or long term. Are you going to evaluate the program once, using a single group of employees? Or do you plan to collect data on a regular basis (e.g., monthly)?

- Identify a minimum acceptable level of effectiveness of your training and development curriculum. What kinds of results do you expect? What will satisfy you and your internal customers?

- Use any measurements of training and development activities that can be converted to dollars (the most effective way to measure ROI).

Complete Activity # 3
The Learning Evaluation Model

Activity 3: The Learning Evaluation Model

For each of the description below, identify which of the four levels of the model they relate to.

	Level
Cognitive outcomes, skill-based outcomes and attitudinal outcomes	
The effect on the business by the trainee	
Evaluation forms or 'smile sheets' are the most common form of evaluation at this level	
The extent of applied learning back on the job	
Measurement of the increase in knowledge before and after	
The enjoyment of the training	
The participants ability to demonstrate newly acquired skills	
Observation is required over time to assess the degree and sustainability of change	
The usefulness of the training	
Measurements linked to the organization's business case	
Measured by assessments before and/or after the training	
Measurement of change typically requires cooperation and skill of line managers	
Bottom-line impact	
What happens to participants after they leave the training room	
Measurement information is collected immediately after the training is completed.	
Measurement information is very quick and easy to obtain.	

Activity # 3 - Check your Answers

Check your work from the previous activity.

	Level
Cognitive outcomes, skill-based outcomes and attitudinal outcomes	2
The effect on the business by the trainee	4
Evaluation forms or 'smile sheets' are the most common form of evaluation at this level	1
The extent of applied learning back on the job	3
Measurement of the increase in knowledge before and after	2
The enjoyment of the training	1
The participants ability to demonstrate newly acquired skills	2
Observation is required over time to assess the degree and sustainability of change	3
The usefulness of the training	1
Measurements linked to the organization's business case	4
Measured by assessments before and/or after the training	2
Measurement of change typically requires cooperation and skill of line managers	3
Bottom-line impact	4
What happens to participants after they leave the training room	3
Measurement information is collected immediately after the training is completed	1
Measurement information is very quick and easy to obtain	1

Now update your Learning Journal (page 65)

MEASURING THROUGH REVIEW

Part 4

The "Review" as a Solid Training Measure

1 What Does a Review Activity Do?

A review activity checks and measures the learning on a particular topic or group of topics while the participants are still in the training room. The purpose of the review activity is to ensure that you are meeting clearly established learning goals and objectives. In order to be truly successful and obtain a true measure of learning, the review activity must have a set outcome for participants. If the standard (or goal) is not set then you will not know when your participants have met it.

The review activity forms the bridge between learning the course content and applying that content in the workplace. It is the first step in the transfer of learning from the classroom to the job.

Benefits of Review to Participants

- Participants gain confidence by showing themselves and others that they are competent.
- Participants refuel and are ready for more content when they are given a structured break in the information flow.
- Participants test-drive new skills in a safe environment, encouraging them to participate freely in activities without the threat of reprimand.

Benefits of Review to Trainers

- The trainer has an opportunity to be a 'fly on the wall' and can observe, listen to and work with participants to check their level of understanding.
- Trainers can observe and respond to gaps in learning.
- Trainers can create an energized group of participants which saves time and keeps learning levels high.
- Trainers can reduce course time by avoiding confusion over content and the need to back-track and re-teach.

Benefits of Review to the Organization

- Review activities greatly enhance the quality of information that is available to the organization as feedback on participant learning levels.
- The review provides data on the standard of participants' knowledge.
- Data can be more easily collated and assessed and consequently fed into the organizations performance management system.

Avoiding Fun for Fun's Sake

A Review activity is not designed to be fun. If fun happens then it might make the review activity more memorable, however fun alone does not instill learning. While fun is great in any training course, a review activity must genuinely review content and participant understanding of that content. Fun for fun's sake is not an effective measure of learning or the potential for workplace application.

What topics are included in a Review?

The topics that are reviewed might range from conceptual to step-by-step process information. For example, in a customer service training course you can review the concepts of getting to know your customers, accepting personal responsibility and valuing difficult customers. Or alternatively you could review steps to enter customer information into a company database, or the seven steps of customer service.

Training Activity vs Review Activity

Training activities are usually conducted immediately after the trainer presents a piece of content to participants. During the training activity learning is still taking place, as the activity directly relates to the content just presented. During training activities the participant is usually doing a fully scripted and guided exercise. In contrast, a review activity is conducted at regular intervals throughout the program to check understanding of larger sections of content. For example, a review may run before and after breaks, post lunch and the conclusion of the program. In a review activity, skills and knowledge are assessed to reassure both trainer and participant that learning transfer has taken place.

How much time does a Review take?

A review activity may be conducted for five minutes or two hours. The duration depends on how much material is being reviewed, and the nature of the success criteria. What is important is that the time invested is appropriate to the amount of content being reviewed. A review activity that takes 30 minutes for participants to complete and reviews only two or three minor points is worthless.

What happens after the Review?

After the review activity, participants should be debriefed. Here, the trainer explores further questions, comments and fills any knowledge gaps of individual participants. To debrief the review well, which includes checking results, asking further questions, and clarifying any outstanding issues, you could expect the debrief to take at least a further five minutes.

Complete Activity # 4
Case Study

Activity 4: Case Study

Sally, a professional training consultant, was recently asked to be involved in the redesign of a series of highly technical computer courses. These courses formed part of a massive technological, organizational, cultural and workplace change initiative. The majority of the programs went for five days continuously. Participants would arrive on Monday, knowing nothing of the new system and by Friday were expected to be competent users. The training room was set up with 15 computers, however the courses typically held 20 participants and there was some sharing of equipment. The trainer, Tim, had himself only just learnt the new system and was doing his best to get participants through the material in time for the organization wide launch.

To ensure that participants would be able to use the new system back on the job, Tim decided to conduct a two-hour closed book exam on the Friday afternoon of each course. The participants were told first thing Monday morning that they would be having an exam on Friday. To balance participant reaction to the exam, Tim also decided to incorporate a fun review into the course. He created an interactive computer game 'Space Wars' to give participants a break from the content. The game was played in teams and was incorporated as a post-lunch review on every day of the program. The review took approximately 30 minutes to run. Points were accumulated throughout the program and the winning team was awarded a prize on Day 5.

Answer the following questions in relation to the case study above.

1. Identify the two different types of review that Tim was attempting to implement during the course?

Activity 4: Continued

Answer the following questions in relation to the case study above.

2. Did Tim consider benefits to the participants, himself (the trainer) and the organization, of running these types of reviews? If yes, explain how. If not, why not?

3. If you were Sally, what recommendations would you make to Tim the improve learning measurement during the course?

Now update your Learning Journal (page 65)

Types of Review Activities

The number and type of reviews available to trainers is boundless and can range from a handout, a card sort, a puzzle, a board game to a competition. Some take little or no preparation, while others require more lead time.

A review activity may be as simple as 'squad challenge' where the trainer asks participants in small groups to develop questions to ask an opposing team of participants. This takes no preparation on the trainer's part, but is an excellent way to review the content both for the questioning team and the answering team. The questioning team is reviewing the content when composing questions; the answering team is reviewing content by coming up with the answers.

Alternatively, the review may be more complex and require pre-preparation of materials, for example a board game activity. Many commercially available games have boards that can easily be adapted for a learning review. In this scenario the trainer needs to clearly understand the rules, develop their own questions, and facilitate the game effectively on their own. Preparation may take 30 minutes to several hours, but once the activity has been developed it can be used time and time again, making it a wise investment in preparation time.

The type of review used in any training program depends largely on the complexity of the content to be reviewed, the time available for review (ie. mini or major review) and the learning expectations. Following are some suggested reviews, how to use them, and where they can be used.

Six of the Best Reviews

1. True / False

Learning Outcome

Participants sort cards of true or false statements into order by engaging in a whole-group discussion about the validity of each statement.

Overview

A whole-group review activity of 10 or more statements that are either true or false.

Where to use

This activity can be slotted into a training course for use almost anywhere during the day.

Steps to Create

- Write statements onto cards or use PowerPoint to create each statement on a separate slide for printing.
- Create two heading cards – true and false.

Steps to Run

- Hand out cards to participants.
- Have them work together to establish whether each statement is true or false then stick them on the wall under the appropriate heading.
- When they have finished go through all statements – false cards first. If the answer is false, ask 'what would make this statement true?' If the answer is true, ask 'why' and 'what if' questions to add depth to the learning.

2. Definition Match

Learning Outcome

To ensure that participants know the definitions of important terms used throughout the course.

Overview

A whole-group activity where participants match cards with terms and definitions. Each participant is given at least one card to ensure that everyone is involved.

Where to use

Any time, however particularly good as end-of-session, start-of-session, post-lunch review.

Steps to Create

- Choose 10 key terms and write definitions for them.
- Create cards in two colors.
- Choose a color for terms; write them or print them on the cards.
- Use the other color to write or print the definitions.
- Create a heading card that says 'term' and another that says 'definition'.

Steps to Run

- Hand out cards to participants until all participants have at least one card.
- Have participants stick the terms and definitions in order under the heading cards.
- When they have finished go through all terms and definitions. If they are correct, then further questioning and discussion can take place to add depth to the learning.

3. Learning Journals

Learning Outcome

To have participants reflect on their learning and how they will apply their knowledge and skills.

Overview

An individual activity where participants are given a learning log or learning journal that they regularly update throughout the course. Time is given to participants for quite, reflective analysis of their key learnings and how they will apply them.

Steps to Create

- Create a section in the participant guide with the headings 'Key Learnings' and 'How will I apply my key learnings'.
- Call this the Learning Log or Learning Journal.

Steps to Run

- At various times of the day give participants some quiet time to consolidate their learning in their learning log or journal.
- Have participants update their learning log or journal regularly throughout the course (either before or after a break, or at the end of each major section of learning).

4. Post Cards of Learning

Learning Outcome

To have participants reflect on their learning and how they will apply their knowledge and skills.

Overview

An individual activity where participants write a postcard about their key learning from each major section of content. They then 'post' the postcard to themselves. They receive their postcards after the training as a reminder of their learnings and a kick start to their action plan.

Where to use

It is important to give participants 5 to 10 minutes of quiet time at least three times a day to complete postcards.

Steps to Create

- Create standard format postcards for each major section or learning.
- On the front put the topic name and an identifying graphic.
- Create a mailbox. A cardboard box covered in paper will suffice.

Steps to Run

- At the end of each major section give participants time to write a postcard to themselves to consolidate their learning.
- Give suggestions on what to write eg. How the topic might be actioned, potential obstacles and how you could overcome them etc.
- Encourage participants to use a variety of styles (written, symbols etc)
- Have them address the postcard to themselves and put it in the mailbox.
- After the course has finished, sort out the postcards by participant, put into a sealed envelope and post two weeks after the completion of the program. Include a sustaining activity or a reminder about the next stage of learning.

> "I don't think much of a man who is not wiser today than he was yesterday."
>
> Abraham Lincoln

5. Step mix

Learning Outcome

To ensure that participants are confident in the correct sequence of a step-by-step procedure.

Overview

Participants are given cards bearing a single step of the process. They place the cards on the training room wall in order. To add depth to the review, two or more step-by-step processes can be jumbled up.

Where to use

Start-of-session, end-of-session, post-lunch etc.

Steps to Create

- Write the steps of a process on separate sheets of card.
- Have masking tape at hand.
Steps to Run.
- Give participants one or two cards each until all are distributed.
- Have participants form the step-by-step process.
- Stick the cards to the wall in order.

6. Money Bags (Jeopardy)

Learning Outcome

To ensure that participants know the key learning points of the training course and to re-energize the group in a fun and competitive way.

Overview

In teams, participants 'beat the buzzer' to answer 12 questions correctly. A board of 12 money bags is divided into three categories. Behind each bag is a question; the higher the dollar value, the more difficult the question.

Where to use

Anytime, but particularly good at end-of-day or end-of-course.

Steps to Create

- Using a piece of heavy flipchart paper or poster board, create a Money Bags board.
    1. Put the heading 'Money Bags' at the top.
    2. Create three categories of questions (eg. Major sections or the course or generic categories like 'quick ways', 'fast cash', 'tips & tricks' etc).
    3. Create three sets of $100, $250, $350, $500 bags.
    4. Using Velcro dots or tape, stick the money bags to the board.
- Write four questions for each of the three categories. They should range in degree of difficulty. The higher the dollar value the more difficult the question.
- Give participants noise makers (buzzers, mini drums, maracas, etc) to use to 'buzz in' with their answer.

Steps to Run

- Re-group participants into small groups of 3-5.
- Have each group invent a team name to display on their table.
- Give each team a noisemaker.
- Explain the rules of the game:
  1. The aim of Money Bags is to collect as much money as possible.
  2. Each money bag has a question associated with it.
  3. This is a beat-the-buzzer game. Your team needs to buzz in the first in order to get a chance to answer.
  4. A correct answer wins the money. An incorrect answer allows other groups to 'buzz in'.
- Have teams test their buzzer.
- As a team answers correctly, give them the money bag.
- Award prizes and consolation prizes accordingly at the end of the activity.

12 More Review Activities

1. Acronym Alive

- Acronyms used in the course are written on a flipchart, whiteboard or printed on a handout. One letter in each acronym is underlined, e.g. RAM. Participants define the underlined letter.
- Acronym Alive is quick to run so use it as a post-lunch review or an end of session review.
- The process of identifying one of the letters in the review forces participants to identify all of the letters.

2. Acronyms Defined

- Run throughout the entire course, this review constantly reminds participants of the definition of acronyms used within the training course.
- A flipchart headed "Acronyms Defined" is created and hung on the wall. At the end of each session, before a break, the trainer and participants update the flipchart with acronyms and their meanings that were discovered during that session.
- This is a great review for technical training where acronyms are often used. Also, this review is fabulous for induction training.

3. Ad Campaign

- Participants 'sell' their key learning point to the rest of the group in the form of a newspaper advertisement.
- Participants review the entire course and make a list of their key learnings.
- From this list they choose their #1 key learning.
- Each participant is given a large sheet of paper on which to draw an advertisement for a magazine or newspaper selling their #1 key learning.

4. Bingo Search

- Each participant is given a handout with 12 questions on it.
- Participants must interview others in the group to find the answers. The participant who can get answers to all questions first shouts "bingo" and is awarded a prize.

5. Concentration (The Memory Game)

- Twenty cards in two colors are laid facedown on the table. One color is for terms, the other for definitions.
- Teams take turns in turning one term and definition card looking for a match. The team with the most matches wins.

6. Crossword Race

- A team review where teams race to complete a crossword of questions from the training course.
- This review activity is simply a disguised test of approximately 40 questions.

7. Fast 7 - Truth or Lies

- An individual review activity of seven statements that is either true or false.
- This is a review activity that can be 'slotted into' a training course for use almost anywhere during the day.

8. Getting Better

- The trainer prepares two or three questions as a handout, on a flipchart or in the participant workbook. Individually participants answer the questions and share their answers in small teams or the whole group.

9. Hangman Rules!

- A whole group activity that has participants in up to four teams.
- Using a beat the buzzer format, participants race to answer the question first and correctly to be awarded with a part of their 'hangman'.

10. Sequence Shuffle

- This is a 'physical form' of step-mix. Participants are given cards on which is written one step of a process.
- In a circle they form the correct sequence of the steps. The trainer then has the opportunity of asking 'why' and 'what if' questions about the sequence.

11. Squad Challenge

- In small groups participants create 10 questions or true/false statements.
- Each 'squad' challenges other 'squads' to answer. The aim is to 'stump the opposing squad'.

12. Wordfinder

- Using a crossword maker or Wordfinder computer software package create a puzzle where the key terms of the course are 'hidden' in the puzzle. Words can run horizontally, vertically, backwards or forwards. Usually the letters remaining will form a key term of the training course.

Different Levels of Review

Review activities can be designed for individual participants, pairs, small groups or large groups. A mix of different review activities provides variety for the participants and the trainer, and more importantly, different levels of participation help to support and provide for individual learning styles.

A mix of whole-group, team-based, pair-and-share, individual and metacognitive (or reflective) reviews should be in every training course, regardless of duration or participant job title and experience.

Whole Group Reviews

Only a very confident and skilled trainer would be likely to choose to run a whole-group review activity. In a whole-group activity all the participants together are involved in a single task, not as separate teams or pairs. Whole group sizes could range from six people to 600, or even more. These activities require careful facilitation to ensure that all participants are involved. Furthermore, a whole-group activity is more difficult to measure, because it is easier for quiet participants to blend in while more outgoing participants take the spotlight. Whole-group activities are excellent when guided by the trainer, but can become unruly if unsupervised. This level of review is recommended for a maximum group size of 12 participants.

1 Team Based Review Activities

The ideal size of a team or group when conducting a review is five.
Any more than five often means that the dominant participants take over, leaving shy and reserved participants on the outside. Any fewer than three in a team activity and the sharing of information may become restrained because the participants don't have enough ideas to work from within the group. It is important for the trainer to supervise the teams, taking note of what each participant is contributing.

Pair-and-Share Review Activities

Pair-and-share reviews are excellent for prompting the sharing of information and are generally less active than team-based reviews. This style of cooperative review has become increasingly popular in training because of its excellent outcomes. Pair-and-share reviews foster close working relationships between participants and puts the trainer in a better position to measure the progress of each participant.

Individual Review Activities

Individual review activities are completed in the training room with free communication and interaction with other participants. An individual review is a classic twist on questions and answers, true-or-false, short answer statements etc presented in a non-exam environment.

Metacognitive Review Activities

Metacognitive[1] reviews are reflective by nature and focus on the application of the material learnt. They challenge participants to think about their thinking. These activities also enable the participant to begin actively constructing meaning - making sense of the world by connecting new learning with what is already known. These are vital connections participants must make in order to apply their learning. Learning journals, hot tips, participant postcards etc are examples of metacongitive reviews.

---

[1] You'll find more information about Metacognition in The Performance Company's – Adult Learning Principles 3 - Advanced Adult Learning Principles.

Balancing Adult Learning Styles

1 A balanced approach means that different styles of review are presented at different times throughout the course. This mix could include (VAK)[2] visual, auditory, kinesthetic and reflective activities. So that you adopt a balanced approach when choosing a mix of review activities, one thing should remain uppermost in your mind: how YOU learn as the trainer is not important. You need to accommodate all types of learners, who may or may not learn in the same way as you.

Style of Learner	Inclusions in Review activities that support learning style
VISUAL	- Spot the error activities where participants have to identify errors in content (written materials such as case studies, handouts etc). - General use of color and pictures eg. Cards with true or false statements, fill-in-the-gaps, handouts, flipcharts and well illustrated reviews. - Puzzles in which the final picture completes a step-by-step process.
AUDITORY	- Telling others what they have learned. - Listening to an audio cassette or video as a case study. - Listening to 'Hot Tips' from other participants. - Rhythmic learning to learn key concepts or a series of steps in a process.
KINESTHETIC	- Physically sorting cards into different categories (eg, true/false, terms/definitions etc). - Board games in which the teams compete. - Puzzles and jigsaws, in which participants can be actively involved. - Use of Role-Play as a skill practice.

[2] These introductory principles are addressed in The Performance Company's Learning Short-take®: Adult Learning Principles 1 – Engaging the Adult Learner.

Accommodating Several Learning Styles at Once

Working Case Study: Negotiation Skills

Always remember that most review activities support several learning styles at once. Imagine you are training a course on negotiation skills and have decided to have a lively review activity immediately following lunch. You decide to use a crossword puzzle. Immediately we know that a crossword puzzle is aimed at the visual learner; however, with some simple changes many other styles can be accommodated as well. Some of these changes include:

- Enlarging the A4 size crossword into two flip-chart size crossword puzzles and mounting them on the wall.
- Providing each participant with a clue sheet.
- Creating two teams who race each other to complete their own giant team crosswords.

These changes have now broadened the appeal to include kinesthetic and auditory learners (team-based crossword) as well as visual learners (giant poster-size crosswords).

Complete Activity # 5
Training Review Analysis

Activity 5: Training Review Analysis

1

 Download the TPC Training Review Analysis tool from the TPC website at **www.tpc.net.au/tools**

Activity using the TPC Training Review Analysis

Choose an existing real-life training program that you either train now or have been assigned to train in the future. Analyze the type, level and balance of review activities that are currently used in the program.

Now update your Learning Journal (page 65)

BRINGING IT TOGETHER

Part 5

Bringing it Together

1 **Quick Tips for Effective Learning Measurement**

1. Organizations pay for their people to attend training. In return they expect learning goals to be achieved, a behavior change to take place, and a positive bottom-line impact for their investment.
2. Learning can be measured during and following a training program - Kirkpatrick's Learning Evaluation Model - Reaction/Learning/Behavior/Results.
3. A written test or exam does not measure learning. An evaluation form does not measure learning.
4. Review activities are a fundamental form of measurement in any training program.
5. Review activities benefit the participant, the trainer, and the organization.
6. Reviews are not about 'fun for fun's sake'.
7. The range of review activities available to trainers are limitless and can take anything from no preparation to considerable preparation.
8. Review activities should be completed at regular intervals throughout the program for each session of content.
9. Review activities can be undertaken on an individual basis, pair-and-share, small group, or whole-group basis.
10. A balanced approach to review activities is critical in accommodating all adult learning styles.

Complete Activity # 6
Quick Tips

Activity 6: Quick Tips

Pick your top three review tips from the Quick Tips list and describe how you will implement these in your training programs

Quick Tips	How I will implement this tip

Now update your Learning Journal (page 65)

"The purpose of learning is growth, and our minds, unlike our bodies, can continue growing as we continue to live."

Mortimer Adler

Section 2
LEARNING JOURNAL

The Learning Journal is used throughout the Learning Short-take® process to record your key learnings, hot tips and things to remember.

Update your Learning Journal at anytime throughout the Learning Short-take® process. Ensure you complete your Learning Journal after you finish each activity. Then turn back to the Participant Guide to continue your learning.

Learning Journal

As you work through this Learning Short-take®, make detailed notes on this page of the lessons you have learned and any useful skill areas. For each lesson or refresher point think about how you could further develop this skill. Your coach will want to discuss these with you in your Skill Development Action Planning meeting.

"…that is what learning is.
You suddenly understand something you've understood all your life, but in a new way."
Doris Lessing

"Act as though it were impossible to fail."
Winston Churchill

"The wise do at once what the fool does later."
Baltasar Gracian (1601-58), Spanish Jesuit priest and author.

Learning or Idea	Action to be taken	Result Expected

Learning Journal - continued

Learning or Idea	Action to be taken	Result Expected

"Anyone who stops learning is old, whether at twenty or eighty."
Henry Ford

Learning or Idea	Action to be taken	Result Expected

2

"Do not be too timid and squeamish about your actions. All life is an experiment.
The more experiments you make the better. What if they are a little course, and you may get your coat soiled or torn?
What if you do fail, and get fairly rolled in the dirt once or twice. Up again, you shall never be so afraid of a tumble."

Ralph Waldo Emerson

Section 3

SKILL DEVELOPMENT ACTION PLAN

Your Skill Development Action Plan is the last Step in the Learning Short-take® process. After you have completed the Participant Guide and all Activities update your Learning Journal then complete this section.

Skill Development Action Plan

This is the most important part of the program - your individual Skill Development Action Plan.

You need to complete this plan before meeting with your manager or prior to on-going coaching. You will discuss it in detail with your manager or coach as he or she will ensure that you have everything you need to complete the tasks and activities.

Once you have completed your **Skill Development Action Plan** schedule a meeting time with your manager or coach to review your plan. Take your participant guide and all other documentation received during the training course to this meeting.

Remember - you have committed to your **Skill Development Action Plan**, and need to make time to complete your tasks!

> "The mind, once stretched by a new idea, never regains its original dimensions."
> Oliver Wendell Holmes

> "Whatever you can do or dream you can - begin it. Boldness has genius, power and magic."
> Johann Wolfgang von Goethe

"Imagination is the eye of the soul."
Joseph Joubert (1754-1824)

Task or activity (Be specific)	Measure (this will help you to know you have achieved it)	Date (Be specific)
Reflect on your Learning Journal. Transfer action items that you can apply to your job. Ensure that you include some 'stretch goals' and also a blend of short, medium and long term goals.	Apart from you, who else is needed to assist you in achieving your goal.	Be specific. A general date such as 'Quarter 1', 'August', or 'by end of year' is vague and more likely to result in not achieving your target. Be specific – e.g. 22nd November.

Ideas for discussion with my manager

Ideas

Congratulations!

You've now completed this Learning Short-take®.

Meet with your Manager/Coach to discuss your Skill Development Action Plan.

Suggested Reading

Mattiske, Catherine, 2001. Train for Results. Maximise the Impact of Training Through Review. Allen & Unwin.

American Society of Training & Development (ASTD). 2000. Why ROI? - Return on Investment - Brief Article.

Kirkpatrick, Donald, L. (1998) Evaluating Training Programs. The Four Levels.

Phillips, Jack, J. (2003) Return on Investment in Training and Performance Improvement Programs. Butterworth-Heinemann

"There are precious few Einsteins among us. Most brilliance arises from ordinary people working together in extraordinary ways."

Roger Von Oech

QUICK REFERENCE

This Quick Reference provides you with a summary of key concepts, models and reference material from Learning Short-takes®. We have also included some quotations to ponder.

Use this section as a quick reference to keep your learning active.

Quick Reference

The first step to measuring learning

To facilitate a positive bottom-line result, it is important to first understand how learning can be effectively measured in the classroom. It is during the training event itself that we have the first opportunity to observe learning transfer taking place.

> **You don't understand anything until you learn it more than one way.**
>
> Marvin Minsky

Quick Reference

Common Myths About Measuring Training in the Classroom

Myth 1: Learning Can't be Measured During a Training Course

Myth 2: A Written Test or Exam Measures Learning

Myth 3: An Evaluation Form is a Measure of Learning

Myth 4: There is no time left in the course for review

> **We learn more by looking for the answer to a question and not finding it than we do from learning the answer itself.**
>
> Lloyd Alexander

Quick Reference

Kirkpatrick's Learning Evaluation Model

Level 1 - Reactions and Planned Action

Level 2 - Learning

Level 3 - Behavior

Level 4 - Results

Level 5 - Return on Investment (ROI) - Jack Phillips

Level 1: Reactions and Planned Action

Question: How did participants respond to the training?

- Enjoyment of training (emotional reaction) - "I found this training program to be enjoyable."

- Usefulness of training (perceived value) - "What level of value does the training content have for your job?"

- Difficulty of training - "I found the issues taught in training difficult to understand."

Quick Reference

Level 2: Learning

4

Question: To what extent did participants experience changes in attitudes, skills, or motivations as a result of the training?

- Cognitive Outcomes
- Skill Based Outcomes
- Attitudinal Outcomes

Level 3: Behavior

Question: Can behavior change be observed on the job as a result of training (i.e., learning transfer)?

- Post-course assessment
- Observed behavior change
- Performance monitoring
- Comparison to 'control group' i.e. those who haven't completed any training

Quick Reference

Level 4: Results

Question: How have organizational outcomes changed as a result of the training program?

- Productivity
- Customer satisfaction
- Efficiency
- Morale
- Profitability

Level 5: Return on Investment (ROI) - Jack Phillips

Question: Did the benefits of training outweigh the costs?

- Calculated cost of training intervention vs. Return on Investment
- Behavior change converted to monetary values
- Training must exceed the potential value of alternative investments
- Show cause-and effect relationships between training and ROI

Quick Reference

4

> **Beware of the man who works hard to learn something, learns it, and finds himself no wiser than before.**
>
> Kurt Vonnegut, Jr.

The "Review" as a Solid Training Measure

Quick Reference

Types of Review Activities

- Start of Day Review

- End of session review (i.e. before a break)

- Start of session review (i.e. after a break)

- Post-lunch review

- End of day review-End of course review

Six of the Best Reviews

1. True / False

2. Definition Match

3. Learning Journals

4. Post Cards of Learning

5. Step mix

6. Money Bags (Jeopardy)

Quick Reference

12 More Review Activities

1. Acronym Alive
2. Acronyms Defined
3. Ad Campaign
4. Bingo Search
5. Concentration
6. Crossword Race
7. Fast 7 - Truth or Lies
8. Getting Better
9. Hangman Rules!
10. Sequence Shuffle
11. Squad Challenge
12. Word Finder

> **I am always ready to learn although I do not always like being taught.**
>
> Winston Churchill

Quick Reference

Different Levels of Review

- Whole Group Reviews
- Team Based Review Activities
- Pair-and-Share Review Activities
- Individual Review Activities
- Metacognitive Review Activities

4

> " I have never in my life learned anything from any man who agreed with me. "
>
> Dudley Field Malone

Quick Reference

Balancing Adult Learning Styles

4

Choose Review Activities that incorporate:

- Visual

- Auditory

- Kinesthetic

> **I don't think much of a man who is not wiser today than he was yesterday.**
>
> Abraham Lincoln

4

"Personal power is the ability to take action."

Anthony Robbins

NEXT STEPS

Congratulations! You have now completed this Learning Short-take® title. The entire list of Learning Short-takes® can be found on the TPC website.

In this section we have suggested Learning Short-take® titles for you that will build your learning. You may order these Learning Short-takes® online at www.tpc.net.au or from your bookstores.

Adult Learning Principles 1
Understanding the Ways Adults Learn

Learning Short-take® Outline

Adult Learning Principles 1 combines self-study with realistic workplace activities for trainers, educators, facilitators and managers to develop skills and knowledge in the principles of adult learning. It will add adult learning techniques to your 'grab bag' of learning design tools for improved learning outcomes. After evaluation of your current approach to learning design, you will learn to develop new and innovative strategies to engage learners at every level. Significantly increasing participant retention and training results **Adult Learning Principles 1** will fuel your confidence in designing successful training workshops and e-Learning every time.

The principles of adult learning work on the basis that we all learn differently, and the way we like to receive and interpret information varies from person to person. Trainers and facilitators who use a combination of adult learning principles to provide balance in their programs increase the chances of keeping all participants focused and engaged throughout the learning process. **Adult Learning Principles 1** will assist you in building a good mix of adult learning styles which is critical in ensuring learning, thorough participant retention and workplace application.

Adult Learning Principles 1 includes the **Adult Learning Principles Quick Reference Wall Chart**, provided as a free downloadable tool.

Learning Objectives

- Successfully match adult learning terms with definitions.
- Determine your personal Learning Style preference.
- List and give working examples of three Adult Learning Principles – Global vs Specific, Learning Styles and Learning Types.
- Develop strategies and ideas to link Adult Learning Principles with Instructional Design.

Course Content

- Part 1: Understanding Adult Learners
- Part 2: Adult Learning Principle 1 - Global vs Specific Learners
- Part 3: Adult Learning Principle 2 - Learning Style - Modalities
- Part 4: Adult Learning Principle 3 - Learning Types - The 4Mat System

Adult Learning Principles 3
Advanced Adult Learning Principles

Learning Short-take® Outline

Adult Learning Principles 3 combines self-study with realistic workplace activities to build advanced knowledge of adult learning principles. Building on Adult Learning Principles 1 and 2, it explores three sophisticated principles of adult learning: Multiple Intelligences, Whole Brain Learning and Metacognitive Reflection. **Adult Learning Principles 3** is designed for educators, trainers and facilitators who work in instructor-led training, e-Learning, distance learning, self-study and other types of learning interventions.

The reliance on just a few training approaches may be a combination of trainer "comfort" and organizational expectations. Often, corporate training represents a school-like environment: lectures followed with an activity. With increasing pressure on training departments to reduce training session duration and convert instructor led training to e-learning, trainers must adopt new ways of delivering learning. This Learning Short-take® will provide a plethora of new ideas and refuel the way you design learning.

Adult Learning Principles 3 includes the **Multiple Intelligence Quick Reference Card**, provided as a free downloadable tool.

Course Content

- Part 1: Whole Brain Learning
  - Brain Dominance
  - Assessing Hemispheric Dominance
- Part 2: Multiple Intelligences
  - Logical-Mathematical Intelligence
  - Musical Intelligence
  - Bodily-Kinesthetic Intelligence
  - Visual/Spatial Intelligence
  - Interpersonal Intelligence
  - Intrapersonal Intelligence
  - Naturalist Intelligence
  - Existential Intelligence
- Part 3: The Metacognitive Process
  - Strategies for Developing Metacognitive Behaviors
  - Journal Writing

Learning Objectives

- Explain the value of using a balanced adult learning approach.
- List the characteristics of left brain dominance vs. right brain dominance.
- Use the Brain Dominance theory to analyze and make improvements to an existing training program.
- List the Multiple Intelligences.
- Analyze an existing training program and suggest improvements to maximize the Multiple Intelligence Balance.
- Define metacognitive reflection and be able to implement learning and review activities using this training method.
- Create a Skill Development Action Plan.

Fast-track Instructional Design
Excellence in Course Development using ID9

Learning Short-take® Outline

Fast-track Instructional Design combines self-study with real workplace activities to provide you with loads of tips, tricks and techniques for writing and creating sensational training courses. You will learn Mattiske's ID9™ process that reduces instructional design time, balances the needs of all learners, and ensures maximum participant retention and application. ID9™will fuel you with new ideas and recharge your enthusiasm for course design.

A sound instructional design process is critical to training success and learning retention. The instructional design process dictates the flow of the training program and, if structured effectively, ensures both trainer and participants achieve program and learning objectives. **Fast-track Instructional Design** introduces ID9™, the 9-step instructional design model, which facilitates program success from a 'great Open' to a 'sensational Close.'

Fast-track Instructional Design includes the **ID9™ Wallchart**, provided as a free downloadable tool.

Learning Objectives
- Write clear and concise course goals.
- Write results oriented learning objectives using action verbs.
- Demonstrate practical use of the 9-step Instructional Design model in course development.
- Create a smooth-flowing session opening, including the Welcome, Icebreaker, Agenda, Objectives, and Connect Activity.
- Work with all types of content and create interactive learning sessions with sound adult learning processes.
- Design training that will ensure participant interaction.
- Write effective review activities and closing phase to all training.
- Create a Skill Development Action Plan.

Course Content
- Part 1: About Instructional Design
- Part 2: The 9-Step ID Process - Overview
- Part 3: Create the Opening
- Part 4: Create Training Modules
- Part 5: Create the Learning Check
- Part 6: Create the Close
- Part 7: Create Materials

TPC - The Performance Company is known world wide as 'the place to go' for Corporate Training Courses, e-Learning, Train the Trainer and Instructional Design Programs.

Corporate Training Division

> Global Learning Platform - Coordinate your training worldwide
> Instructional Design - Customized instructor-led and e-Learning courses for your organization
> Trainer Development - Maximize your training effectiveness
> Coaching - Get the best from your participants
> Strategic Consulting - Helping clients meet their goals

Learning Short-takes® Division

> Professional Development
> Sales and Customer Service
> Leadership and Management
> Trainer Development
> Able to be customized for individual clients

www.tpc.net.au